DATE DUE

About

Michael

Jackson

James

Haskins

ENSLOW PUBLISHERS, INC.

Bloy St. & Ramsey Ave.   P.O. Box 38
Box 777   Aldershot
Hillside, N.J. 07205   Hants GU12 6BP
U.S.A.   U.K.

Library of Congress Cataloging in Publication Data

Haskins, James, 1941-
    About Michael Jackson.

    Discography: p.
    Includes index.
    Summary: Discusses the life, career, and music of the
pop singer who began performing with his family and went
on to become a highly successful solo act.
    1. Jackson, Michael, 1958-   —Juvenile literature.
2. Rock musicians—United States—Biography—Juvenile litera-
ture. [1. Jackson, Michael, 1958-   . 2. Singers. 3. Afro-
Americans—Biography. 4. Rock music] I. Title.
ML3930.J25H34 1985 784.5'4'00924 [B] [92] 84-26036
ISBN 0-89490-112-5

Printed in the United States of America

10 9 8 7 6 5 4 3 2 1

Illustration Credits
AP/Wide World Photos, pp. 30, 47, 55, 85; United Press
International Photos, pp. 4, 16, 19, 27, 41, 49, 61, 63, 68,
75, 80, 82, 90.

Contents

Michael and E.T. Steven Spielberg, who created E.T., says, "If E.T. hadn't come to Elliott, he would have come to Michael's house."

1

$\mathcal{M}$ichael Jackson's Planet

"If E.T. hadn't come to Elliott, he would have come to Michael's house." That's what movie director Steven Spielberg, the creator of E.T., says about Michael Jackson. He is probably right. At Michael's house there are a llama named Louie, two fawns named Prince and Princess, a ram named Mr. Tibbs, a boa constrictor, three parrots, two pairs of swans, and some peacocks. Michael has an old-fashioned outdoor popcorn machine and an ice cream-making machine. In the house, where he lives with his mother and sister LaToya, there is a game room full of video arcade games like Frogger, Space Invaders, and Pac-Man. Another room contains a smaller version of the Disneyland ride Pirates of the Caribbean. Michael also has a sixteen-track recording studio and a complete movie screening room with a huge collection of movies, including many Walt Disney films, 1940s Fred Astaire movies, and *E.T.* Yes, E.T. would probably like it at Michael's house.

He would probably also like Michael. Michael certainly likes
E.T. He has watched the film over and over, never losing the
sense of adventure and wonder. He still cries over the sad scenes.
When he narrated the E.T. storybook album he kept crying at
the point of the story when E.T. is supposed to be dying. While
working on the narration he met the E.T. character, and he
talked to it as if it really was a little creature from outer space.
Michael has no trouble at all believing in things that other people
would call fantasy. He believes that people could fly if we could
"think the right thoughts and levitate ourselves off the ground."
Says Quincy Jones, producer of his smash-hit record albums,
"Sometimes I think Michael's from another planet."

Michael Peters, who does the choreography for Michael's
videos, says, "I think he's really Peter Pan. He is this constant
dichotomy of man and child. He can run corporations and tell
record companies what he wants, and then he can sit in a trailer
and play Hearts for hours with a friend who is twelve years old."

His fans are as young as four years old. They may not know
what his last name is, but they know he is "Michael" and they
want to wear a button with his picture on it. There probably
isn't a high school student in the country who hasn't at least
heard of him. After he won eight Grammy Awards in March 1984,
several students at a high school in Bound Brook, New Jersey,
showed up at school wearing single white gloves. When the
principal banned the wearing of white gloves, the school was
in an uproar. Newspapers and radio stations across the United
States and in Canada carried the story.

Older people like him, too. Many people in their thirties and
forties watched the 1983 TV special celebrating Motown's 25th
anniversary because they wanted to see the Motown acts that
were popular in the 1960s. But by the end of the show, all they

could talk about was Michael Jackson. One of Michael's biggest fans is Katharine Hepburn, who is over seventy. The only pop music concert she has ever been to was a Jacksons concert.

People in foreign countries have bought so many copies of Michael's album *Thriller* that it is now in the *Guinness Book of World Records* as the album with the highest international sales in history. Many of these people do not speak much English and have no idea what the lyrics of Michael's songs are all about. But they respond to his sound and his personality the same way Americans do. In fact, he is so popular around the world that he has the Russians worried. Most of the time the leaders of the Soviet Union do not pay much attention to American pop stars. But in their opinion Michael Jackson has so much influence over teenagers the world over that he is dangerous. In June 1984 the Kremlin, the Soviet seat of government, charged that his music was "characteristic of that ill-famed American lifestyle which the U.S.A. is trying to foist on the world." Soviet officials said that Michael was "mesmerizing Americans and keeping them from thinking about political things."

Since Michael's music is banned in the Soviet Union, many Russians have no idea what all the fuss is about. But many others have probably heard his records, which they manage to get the same way they manage to get American blue jeans—in the underground market. More than a few have probably also seen Michael's *Thriller* video. One Russian official who had seen it in a foreigner's apartment called it "fascist." That word usually refers to a government or ruler who has complete power over the people. He explained, "This film is really fascist because it forces you to appreciate it like a drug. You were all sitting round obsessed with it—you couldn't even talk to each other." (Sure, Michael wanted his video to have a powerful effect on people, but one wonders what he thought when he learned that a Russian called it "fascist."!)

When Russian officials denounce an entertainer, it's a sure thing that the entertainer is important. Michael Jackson is one of the most famous people in the whole world. He is a multi-multi-millionaire. And he is not even thirty years old. No wonder he believes in fairy tales. His whole life has been like a fairy tale in many ways. What is amazing about his story is that he was not brought to earth by spaceship or on the wings of an eagle. He was born, just like the rest of us, into a perfectly ordinary family, in Gary, Indiana.

2

$\mathcal{A}$n Ordinary Family With a Special Dream

Michael Jackson's life was very ordinary at the start. He was the seventh of nine children born to Joe and Katherine Jackson, a hardworking couple. Neither parent had more than a high school education. But both parents had very strong ideas of family.

Joe Jackson had grown up in Tennessee. He had moved to Gary because there were more jobs there. As a teenager, he went to work in the steel mills as a crane operator. He was a talented guitar player and got together with other musicians he met as often as he could. His dream was to be an entertainer, but he never had much chance to follow that dream. In 1949 when he was twenty-one, he married a pretty eighteen-year-old from outside Chicago named Katherine. They started a family right away, and as the years passed and children began to arrive, Joe Jackson's dreams of a career in music were pushed farther and farther into the back of his mind. For a while after his marriage he played in and around Chicago with a band called the Falcons. But the Falcons never went beyond playing one-night stands at college parties and bars. According to Joe Jackson, "We tried to be professional, but we couldn't get the right type of management, guidance, or contacts, so we never really did anything serious with it." After a while Joe Jackson played his guitar only for his family and friends. His electric guitar was his most prized possession, and he would not let any of his children touch it.

There were more and more children as the years went by. Maureen came first, then Sigmund Esco (nicknamed Jackie), then Toriano Adaryl (Tito), then Jermaine La Jaune, then LaToya, then Marlon. Michael Joe was born August 29, 1958, followed by Steven Randall (Randy) and Janet.

The family lived on Jackson Street, and that seems fitting. With all those children, there were probably more Jacksons on the street than anyone else. The house only had three bedrooms, so there was a lot of doubling—and tripling and quadrupling—up. There wasn't much privacy in the Jackson household. Family togetherness was something they could not avoid. But Katherine Jackson worked hard to make that family togetherness a happy thing. Her religion said that a family should be together. She was, and still is, a Jehovah's Witness, and Jehovah's Witnesses place great store in family closeness. Joe Jackson was brought up a Baptist, but the children were raised in his wife's religion. They went to services three times a week at the local Kingdom Hall. The children were taught that the second coming of Christ had already begun and that He had brought a higher order than earthly governments. They were taught to follow the strict moral codes of the Witnesses above any governmental laws.

While Katherine Jackson was mainly responsible for her children's religious upbringing, Joe Jackson had a lot to say in their everyday lives. He encouraged his boys to play sports and to be in team sports at school. In doing so, he also encouraged togetherness. Both parents liked to gather the whole family around to listen to records and to make music themselves. Joe Jackson would play his guitar, Katherine Jackson the piano, and all the children would sing. They sang "You Are My Sunshine" and "Cotton Fields" and current pop hits. Joe and Katherine remarked to each other how good the children's voices were. They encouraged all the children who showed interest in the piano. But whenever one of his sons picked up his guitar, Joe Jackson was not encouraging at all. His guitar was not a toy, he told them. He didn't want them playing around with it.

Katherine Jackson says that there were never any real problems disciplining the children. "After you instill in the two oldest what they can and cannot do, the others automatically follow," she has said. Unfortunately, the three oldest boys could not stay away from their father's guitar. It was exciting to sneak into the closet where it was kept and to pluck its forbidden strings. They must have gotten pretty good at it, playing the guitar in secret, for when their father discovered what they had been doing and challenged them, they proved equal to the challenge. Tito was the one who loved the guitar most and who sneaked in to play it most often. One day he broke one of the guitar's strings, and that's how Joe Jackson found out that someone had been playing the instrument.

Michael was only about four at the time, but he remembers what happened. Many years later he told an interviewer for *Crawdaddy*, "My father got so mad, so *angry*, and he said, 'Tito, sit down, I wanna see if you can play that guitar. If you can't, I'm really gonna *beat* you.' " Tito was so scared he was shaking all over, but he played. He played so well that Joe Jackson forgot all about being angry. He was amazed at his son's talent. He soon learned that Jermaine was quite good on the guitar, too. Joe Jackson remembered his own dream of a career in music, and he thought that maybe it could come true for his children.

Joe Jackson decided to form a family band. He went out and bought second-hand instruments, and soon all the older children were practicing. Tito played the guitar. Jermaine, who had the best voice, played bass. Jackie was also on the guitar. Maureen and LaToya accompanied on violin and clarinet. The younger children watched and listened and wished they were old enough to take part. Michael was especially interested in what his older brothers and sisters were doing and was always under foot.

Katherine Jackson had mixed feelings about her husband's family project. She worried that the money used to buy instruments was money they needed for clothes and food. But she liked the idea that all the family were doing something together. And she realized that her husband would not be talked out of following his dream.

Joe Jackson began going to local clubs and dances to watch the musical groups. He made mental notes about which songs they played and sang, what they wore, how they moved around onstage. Back home he would teach his children new songs and new dance steps. Because he felt the band needed an organist and a drummer, he brought in two nephews, Johnny Jackson and Ronnie Rancifer. They already had their own instruments, and Katherine Jackson was grateful for that.

The children practiced for hours every day, but they never played their music outside the house. For years the living room of the Jackson home was their only stage. Joe Jackson believed that practice makes perfect, and when the children finally did play on a real stage he wanted them to be complete professionals.

One reason that this took some years was that the composition of the group kept changing. The girls, Maureen and LaToya, did not show the same interest as the boys, and they eventually dropped out. So did cousin Ronnie. Marlon and Michael replaced them. Michael was only five years old when his father decided to include him. The little boy was a talented mimic, and when he imitated Jermaine singing lead and played the bongo drums at the same time, his father was convinced. In fact, Michael soon took over as lead singer, and none of the other boys minded. Jackie recalls that Michael was "so energetic that at five years old he was like a leader, we saw that. . . .The speed was the thing. He would see somebody do something and he could do it right away." Since the boys were singing songs and doing dances copied from popular groups, the ability to imitate was very important. Katherine Jackson wondered where Michael had gotten so much energy and ability. "It was sort of frightening. He was so young. He didn't go out and play much. So if you want me to tell you the truth, I don't know where he got it. He just *knew*."

Marlon showed great talent as a dancer and became part of the group when he was six. The two younger boys practiced the same long hours as the older boys. Michael remembers coming home from school at three and seeing everything set up in the living room, waiting for them. They would practice until dinner-time, and then practice some more after that. "And we kept on and kept on and had different meetings and stuff, and we used to wonder, When will we have a show?"

In 1965 when Michael was seven, they got their chance at last. Joe Jackson decided that he had taught them all he could at home. They were ready for onstage training. They entered a talent show at local Roosevelt High School.

At the time, Motown Records in Detroit was capturing most of the top spots on the singles charts. Groups like the Temptations, Smokey Robinson and the Miracles, Martha and the Vandellas, and the Supremes had hit after hit. Most black amateur groups copied the Motown acts, and the Jacksons were no exception. For the talent show they chose a recent hit by the Temptations called "My Girl." Katherine Jackson made matching vests for them to wear. Billed as the Jackson Five and Johnny, they walked out onto the stage of the high school auditorium.

"I was scared, of course," Michael has said. "I was scared to let the people see me sing. They might 'boo' us. They might not like us. But I've never been so scared that I wasn't ready." Arranged by size, with the older boys in the center and the little ones on either side, the Jackson Five and Johnny launched into "My Girl." Their voices blended as well, if not better, than the Temptations. On the choruses they danced in unison, using choreographed steps that they had practiced for weeks. Michael sang lead. His high, little-boy voice was as controlled as an adult's. He danced about the stage as if he'd been born there. When they finished the number, the audience whistled and cheered, and they won first prize in the contest.

They entered two other talent shows and walked away with the top prize in both, even though they were up against some pretty stiff competition. Deniece Williams, who is now a star herself, competed against them in one of the contests. After that, Joe Jackson took every chance for the group to perform. They played hospital benefits and shopping centers and high school dances. Their first paying dates were at a local nightclub called Mr. Lucky's. The management paid them between five and eight dollars a night, but they always went home with much more. Michael remembers, "People would throw all this money on the floor, tons of dollars, tens, twenties, lots of change." It was Michael who figured out how to pick up the money without having to stop performing. He made it part of his act. He'd go into a spin, dip down, and scoop up a handful of money. He would do a split, grab another handful of bills, and be up in one smooth movement. The sight of the energetic little boy dancing around, picking up money so delighted the audiences that they threw more, just to watch him. "I remember my pockets being so full of money that I couldn't keep my pants up," says Michael. "I'd wear a real tight belt, and I'd buy candy like crazy."

Soon Joe Jackson was taking his family on the road. On weekends and during school vacations they would pile into a borrowed Volkswagen microbus and set out for Illinois and Wisconsin and Missouri, playing mostly nightclubs. Some of these clubs did not have the proper atmosphere for a group of kids. Michael remembers seeing a stripper perform when he was too young to really understand what was going on. Joe and Katherine Jackson did not like having the children exposed to such things, but Joe believed that the boys had to get experience. Also, he had quit his job as a crane operator in order to devote his time to his sons' career, and the family needed the money they earned at these nightclubs.

After performing all weekend the boys would pile back into the van and head for Gary. Often they would not get home until three or four o'clock in the morning, but they would be up at eight and off to school. And as soon as they got home from school they would have to start practicing. Making it in the music business was hard work, and Joe Jackson never tried to pretend to his sons that it was all just fun. It was a job. In 1977 Michael told a reporter for the *Los Angeles Times*, "It's kind of a shame we didn't grow up doing what other kids did. We had to rehearse every day after school when the other kids

The Jackson Five, about 1966. From left, kneeling: Tito, Jackie, Jermaine. Seated: Marlon and Michael.

were outside playing. Sometimes we could hear all the fun and excitement but we could never join in. We missed trick-or-treating and football games and all that. Sure, we had plenty of things the other kids didn't have, but we had to sacrifice to get those things." Michael's way of keeping the other kids as his friends was to buy them candy. Every week he received an allowance of twenty dollars, and he would buy candy for all the kids in the neighborhood.

By 1967 cousin Johnny had left the group, but that made little difference in their music. They were very popular in Gary and the surrounding area. A local record company called Steeltown (steel was Gary's major industry) gave them a chance to record. Their first single contained a song called "I'm A Big Boy Now," backed by a song called "You've Changed." Michael sang lead on both, with his brothers singing backup or response. "I'm A Big Boy Now" was a hit locally, but Steeltown did not have a system for distributing its records outside the area. A distribution company called Atco picked it up for distribution in the Midwest.

Some months later, the Jackson Five recorded another single for Steeltown. "We Don't Have to Be Over 21 (To Fall in Love)" was backed by "Jam Session," in which Joe Jackson joined the group and played his electric guitar. This record did not do well even in Gary. Joe Jackson decided that it was a waste of time recording with local companies. He wanted to get a contract with a big company, and he sent several tapes to Motown in Detroit. But Motown received hundreds of tapes from hopeful performers each week. The Jackson Five tapes probably got put in a storeroom and were never even listened to.

By 1968 when Michael was ten, the Jackson Five were ranging even farther afield, playing big theaters in the black sections of major cities: the Uptown Theater in Philadelphia, the Howard Theater in Washington, D.C. That summer they were invited to perform at the famous Apollo Theatre in Harlem, and they realized that this could be their big break. If an entertainer or group played the Apollo and the audience liked them, they could be almost sure of success. Apollo audiences were notorious as the toughest audiences in the world. If they didn't like you, they would throw cans and bottles, and would boo and hiss. Every Wednesday night was amateur night. Many hopeful performers never performed again after being booed off the stage. But many other hopefuls were "discovered" at Apollo amateur nights and went on to become famous. Leslie Uggams,

James Brown, Wilson Pickett, Dionne Warwick, and Pearl Bailey all had their careers launched at the Apollo.

Joe Jackson remembers that night. "There was this object just onstage which resembled a tree trunk which was supposed to bring good luck to first-time entertainers if you touched it just before going on. Although the object was . . . just behind the curtain, it was positioned so that most of the audience could see you when you touched it. I remember the kids touching it before they went on. One thing about the Apollo Theatre, if you weren't good, you might get a few cans or bottles thrown at you. The kids were more afraid of that than anything else. We weren't afraid of losing the contest, we knew we had it. We just wanted the people to like us. They went out there and performed, and won; in fact, we got a standing ovation. . . .And from that point on we got invitations to come back to the Apollo Theatre to perform for money."

Gladys Knight and her backup singers, the Pips, were performing at the Apollo at the time. She was so impressed with the Jackson Five that she recommended them to her record label, Motown. Around the same time, Richard Hatcher, who was hoping to be elected the first black mayor of Gary, Indiana, asked Berry Gordy, Motown's president, to send some of his stars to entertain at a fund-raising event. Gordy sent Diana Ross and Bobby Taylor. Hatcher also asked Joe Jackson if his boys would perform, and Jackson agreed. At the fund-raiser, Diana Ross met the Jackson Five and fell in love. She told a reporter for *Newsweek*, "Michael won me over the first moment I saw him. I saw so much of myself as a child in Michael. He was performing all the time. That's the way I was. He could be my son."

The Jackson Five with Diana Ross. Michael had a big crush on Diana, and she loved him as the child she did not have.

The twenty-four-year-old Ross was lead singer of the Supremes, Motown's hottest act at the time. She was also dating Berry Gordy, and when she excitedly told Gordy about the Jackson Five, he sat up and listened. People like Gladys Knight are somewhat resentful that Diana Ross is given all the credit for discovering the Jackson Five. Even Michael has stated that no one but Joe and Katherine Jackson discovered the group. It is likely that they would have made it big anyway. But there is no question that Diana Ross had the most influence over Berry Gordy.

Gordy held a party at his mansion in Detroit. He flew the Jackson Five and Motown's major executives to the party. Many of the Motown artists were there as well. When it came time for the Jackson Five to perform, they felt funny about singing the same songs that these artists had made famous. But everyone loved them, and gave them a standing ovation after they finished performing. Two months later, the Jackson Five had a recording contract with Motown. Their lives would never be the same again.

3

$\mathcal{T}$ he Jackson Family Joins the Motown "Family"

The Jackson Five signed with Motown in the winter of 1968-1969, but Motown did not release their first record until November 1969. Berry Gordy's way of operating was to groom his acts thoroughly before presenting them to Motown's public. Joe Jackson had already spent years training his boys, and he did not feel they needed additional work. After all, they were not a group of kids fresh from the streets of Detroit, as most of Motown's acts had been when Gordy had first signed them. But when you joined the Motown "family" you did what you were told, and Berry Gordy wanted to change a few things about the Jackson Five.

Gordy felt that they should have a more individual style. He thought they imitated other groups too closely. He felt that Michael's choreography, his way of moving and dancing on stage, was too much like that of popular soul singer James Brown. Motown's choreographers worked with the boys for months.

Meanwhile, Motown's makeup people found a special "look" for the boys. In addition to costumes that were more slick than those Katherine Jackson could run up on her Singer sewing machine, this "look" included huge Afro hairstyles, which had become popular by the late 1960s. Finally, the boys were coached on how to behave at interviews. They were always to keep themselves in check, never say anything that might lead to controversy.

The most difficult part of preparing the Jackson Five for their Motown debut was finding the right songs for them. Theirs had to be a fresh sound and a distinctive sound. It had to appeal to the teenage market. It had to include songs sung by an eleven-year-old with the sophistication of an eighteen-year-old. Finding the right songs took longer than any other part of the Motown grooming of the Jackson boys. Michael and his brothers re-corded many songs at the Motown studios before one was re-leased. They found that they had to change the way they sang, too. They had to sing the way the producers wanted them to. But they were so excited about being part of the Motown "family" that they did not mind making these changes.

The family aspect of Motown is almost a legend in itself. Many of the groups were brought to the company by other groups. Several of the artists married into Berry Gordy's family or business. Gordy himself was more than a boss. In many ways, he was like a father to them all. Motown was Gordy and Gordy was Motown.

By the time he signed the Jackson Five to a recording contract, Berry Gordy was spending most of his time in Los Angeles. He used his Detroit mansion mostly for parties. He wanted to produce television shows and movies, and he was setting up a new division of his company in the motion picture capital of

the world. At the time, he planned to keep his recording business in Detroit, but eventually most of the recording operations moved to the West Coast, too. Diana Ross moved to Los Angeles in late 1969, and around the same time so did the Jackson family.

"We always dreamed of going to Hollywood," Michael told an interviewer for *Seventeen* in 1978. "We'd hear 'Live from Hollywood!' on TV, and it would be so exciting. When we actually got there, we just started screaming because it was so pretty. You didn't see palm trees, stars, the Sunset Strip back home in Gary. California was like a dream."

Since the Jacksons did not have enough money to buy a house in California, some of the boys stayed with Berry Gordy and some with Diana Ross. Michael lived with Diana for almost a year and a half. "It was like paradise," he says. "We went to Disneyland, we had fun every day. This was a whole other thing from Gary, Indiana." The two became very close. At age eleven, Michael had a big crush on Diana, and she loved him as the child she did not have. One of the many rumors about Michael Jackson is that he really is her son, but there is no truth to it.

The Jackson Five's first Motown single was released at last in November 1969. Titled "I Want You Back," it featured Michael's amazing young voice. His brothers' backup singing was no more or less important than the guitars and violins. Not only was an eleven-year-old singing a love song to a girl and sounding believable, but also his phrasing and control were like an adult's. Michael didn't see any reason why they shouldn't be. After all, he had been singing since he was five. "I was a veteran before I was a teenager," he says.

The single was first played on selected radio stations in advance of its actual release to record stores. The boys themselves made their television debut on the *Ed Sullivan Show* at the same time that the record was released. In those days, an appearance on the Sullivan TV show was almost guaranteed to bring fame and fortune. Michael's cuteness and energy, and his extraordinary voice, won America's heart. "I Want You Back" was a smash hit.

As soon as the single reached Number One on the charts, Motown released the boys' first album. Titled *Diana Ross Presents The Jackson Five*, it included songs in which other brothers got the chance to sing lead. On their next single, "ABC," Michael again sang lead, but in the call-and-response form of the song his brothers' voices were equally important. It hit Number One on March 14, 1970, and a year later won the group their first Grammy Award. Their second album, also titled *ABC,* was released in early May. Two songs from that album were later released as the two sides of one single: "The Love You Saved," an up-tempo song with Michael at lead, backed by "I Found That Girl," a ballad sung by Jermaine. The record became a double-sided hit in June 1970.

That summer *Third Album* was released. Michael and Jermaine shared the lead on "I'll Be There," the track from the album that became a Number One single. The group featured the songs from *Third Album* on their first major American tour that autumn. They finished the year with *The Jackson 5 Christmas Album*, bringing to a total of four the albums released in 1970. With four hit singles on top of that, it was quite a year for nineteen-year-old Jackie, seventeen-year-old Tito, sixteen-year-old Jermaine, thirteen-year-old Marlon, and twelve-year-old

Michael. Michael once said, "It was like being on a merry-go-round that just kept spinning faster and faster. We just kept racking up hit after hit."

In 1971 the Jackson Five released three more albums and had three more hit singles—"Mama's Pearl," "Never Can Say Goodbye," and "Sugar Daddy." Their names and faces were on T-shirts, stickers, posters, and note pads. They went on a second national tour, appeared on Diana Ross's first solo TV special, *Diana* (she had left the Supremes to go out on her own in 1970), and hosted a TV special of their own. The show's title, *Goin' Back to Indiana*, was also the title of an album and a single. The United States Congress paid tribute to them for their talent and their excellent example to fellow youngsters. They enjoyed a Jackson Day back in Gary where, at a ceremony on 23rd and Jackson Street, their old neighborhood, Jackson Street was to be officially renamed Jackson 5 Street for one week. Unfortunately, there was a blizzard and it never happened.

They had come a long way from the old neighborhood. They now lived in a six-bedroom house in Encino, in the San Fernando Valley near Los Angeles. Even so, the boys had to share bedrooms. It had a swimming pool, a half basketball court, a badminton court, and an archery range. It also had alarms and guard dogs. One of the prices of fame, they were learning, was their loss of privacy. Their first house in California had been in the Hollywood Hills, closer to Los Angeles. But they had also been closer to other celebrities. Their home was on all the tourist maps showing where stars lived. Tour buses and tourists on foot came by all the time to look. Some people even tried to get inside the house. The Jacksons had to go farther away from the city to have any privacy at all. Even farther outside the city, if they didn't have the alarms and dogs, their fans would have broken in at all hours.

Because it was not possible to go out without being recognized and mobbed, the boys stayed at home most of the time when they were not on tour. They grew even closer to one another. They were not only brothers but best friends, playing basketball, swimming, practicing their music. Their best friends outside the family were the sons and daughters of Motown performers and executives, including Berry Gordy, III, and his sister Hazel.

The enthusiasm of their fans also made it impossible for them to go to public school. As Michael once explained, "I only went to one public school in my life [in Gary]. I tried to go to another one here [Los Angeles], but it didn't work, because we'd be in our class and a bunch of fans would break into the classroom, or we'd come out of school and there'd be a bunch of kids waiting to take pictures and stuff like that. We stayed at that school a week. One week! That was all we could take."

When they were in Los Angeles, they attended the Walton School, a small private school. The other kids at the school were the sons and daughters of entertainers and so didn't treat the Jackson boys like stars. On the road, they were accompanied by Rose Fine, a tutor employed by Motown.

They lived in a kind of cocoon or a plastic bubble. They rarely went anywhere alone. When they were interviewed, which was often, a Motown publicist was always present to make sure they did not say anything controversial. In early 1972, Vic Rauseo interviewed the Jackson Five for *Senior Scholastic*. He began by asking if they had done anything for the movement to win civil rights for black people. Many other black entertainers were doing benefits and speaking out on behalf of equal rights for blacks. He was interrupted by Bob

In 1971, two years after their first record for Motown, the Jackson Five performed in their own TV special.

Jones, publicist for Motown: "Hold it right there," Jones said. "They aren't active in any movements, and we don't want you creating any illusions." Jackie, the eldest, who usually spoke for the group, explained, "Look, we appeal to both black and white. . . .We don't make black music or white music, or kid music or adult music; we make our sound for everybody." At twenty, Jackie understood that remarks could get twisted in newspaper and magazine articles. At fourteen, Michael only understood that strangers were not to be trusted.

Fame was hard on all the Jacksons, but it seems to have been especially hard on Michael. An outgoing, energetic little kid when the group first started out, Michael became the brother who was least able to cope with strangers, fans, the outside world. He became the one who most needed the protective bubble, the cocoon. Maybe if he had been just a little bit older, he would not have been so strongly affected.

"Being mobbed hurts," he has said, talking about what happens when he does go out in public. "You feel like you're spaghetti among thousands of hands. They're just ripping you and pulling your hair. And you feel that at any moment you're gonna just break." Outside of his own home, the only place where Michael felt safe, the only place where he could let out all his energy, was on a stage. More than the others, he seemed to thrive on performing—anywhere, anytime, on stages or in recording studios. It is not surprising that he was the first of the Jackson Five to release a solo record.

Drawing on the popularity of "I'll Be There," Michael's solo single was titled "Got To Be There." It was released in October 1971 and remains today one of Michael's favorite records. The album of the same title came out in January 1972, and two more tracks from that album followed the single "Got To Be There" as hits: "Rockin' Robin" and "I Wanna Be Where

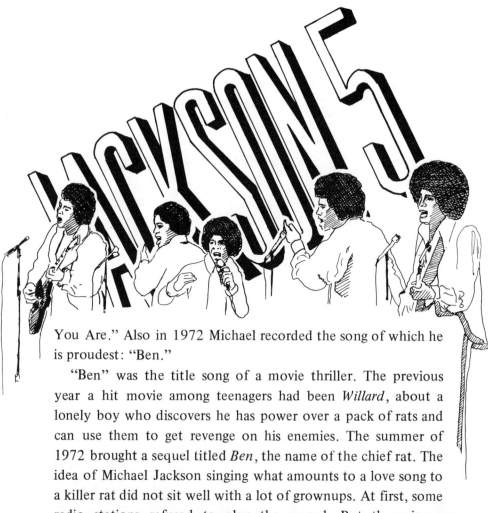

You Are." Also in 1972 Michael recorded the song of which he is proudest: "Ben."

"Ben" was the title song of a movie thriller. The previous year a hit movie among teenagers had been *Willard*, about a lonely boy who discovers he has power over a pack of rats and can use them to get revenge on his enemies. The summer of 1972 brought a sequel titled *Ben*, the name of the chief rat. The idea of Michael Jackson singing what amounts to a love song to a killer rat did not sit well with a lot of grownups. At first, some radio stations refused to play the record. But there is no mention in the song that Ben is a rat, only that he is a true friend. Even if it had, Michael would have been able to sing the song with real feeling. He loved animals—all animals. In fact, he had raised rats himself. When the family had lived in the Hollywood hills, he'd had a cage of rats in the back yard. The record sold well even without radio play, and eventually the radio stations had to play it. It was the first of Michael's solo singles to go platinum (selling more than one million copies), according to Motown. It was also nominated for Best Song at the Academy Awards, and Michael impressed everyone who watched the

At age 13, Michael had amazing poise as a performer. "I was a veteran before I was a teenager," he explained.

awards show on TV. He was a real professional at such a young age. The album *Ben* which followed went gold (selling more than half a million copies), according to Motown. (Since, at that time, Motown would not open its account books to public inspection, none of its gold or platinum records was certified by the record industry; but here, we take their word for it.)

Jermaine Jackson also recorded a solo album late that year. Two singles, "That's How Love Goes" and "Daddy's Home," hit Number 23 and Number 9 on the charts. Handsome Jermaine was the "heartthrob" of the group, and in promoting his solo recordings, Motown pushed him as a black teenage sex symbol.

Meanwhile, there was little easing up on recordings and appearances by the whole group, although the Jackson Five experienced some changes that year. In the late winter Jackie lost control of his Datsun 240Z sports car and hit a parked car, practically destroying both. Jackie escaped injury, but his father forbade him to buy another sports car. In June, eighteen-year-old Tito became the first Jackson boy to marry. Though he and his wife Delores (DeeDee) moved into their own home, it was not far from the family home, and Tito remained with the group.

The Jackson Five produced one album and three singles that year. A television cartoon show, *The Jackson 5*, started in September, although all they did for the show was provide the music: They appeared on television shows and did concerts across the country. In November 1972 they took their first trip abroad.

In England they gave a command performance for the Queen, and for Michael that was one of the greatest thrills of his young life. "Man, there I was, little ole Michael Jackson, shaking hands with the Queen of England. I just felt like flying around the palace." They were nearly as famous in England as they were in the United States, and on that first trip to England they made a very favorable impression on the English as personalities. They were so fresh-faced and clean-cut, so polite. The fact that almost the entire family accompanied the boys—Joe, Katherine, the younger girls, and Tito's new wife DeeDee—helped their all-American image. Randy celebrated his tenth birthday while they were in England. He was a member of the group by then, but sort of unofficially. While he could be found on the drums when the group recorded, his name was not listed on record covers. He would appear in Motown publicity photos, but though there were obviously six people in the picture, it would still be labeled the Jackson Five. Clearly, Motown did not want to tamper with a best-selling name by changing it to the Jackson Six. Young Randy didn't seem to mind. He was just happy to be performing with his brothers.

From England, the Jackson family continued on to mainland Europe, where in France, Germany, and Italy they played to soldout houses. In 1973 they traveled to Australia, New Zealand, and Japan. Motown wanted them to be not just American stars but international stars as well. Why not? By the end of 1972 the Jackson Five had become Motown's most popular act of all time—bigger than Little Stevie Wonder, the Supremes, the Temptations, or any of the others.

But by 1973 the formula that had given them so many hit records suddenly proved no longer to be a winning one. The main problem seemed to be that they were growing up, but their music was not. The three eldest were no longer boys, but men. Jackie tried to prove this with his first solo album, released that year. Titled *Jackie Jackson*, it contained mostly ballads and featured string instruments rather than drums and guitars. He himself described it as "older." It did not sell very well.

None of the Jacksons' records, whether solos or group recordings, sold as well as their recordings of previous years.

The Jackson Five released two albums, *Sky Writer* and *Get It Together*. Neither went gold. Nor did their two singles, "Hallelujah Day" and "Get It Together." Michael's solo album *Music and Me* and solo single "With a Child's Heart" did not do very well either, although his single reached Number 11 on the charts. Jermaine did one notch better with his single "You're in Good Hands."

There were several other reasons why their recordings were not doing so well. One was that the Motown team that had written and produced most of their previous hits had broken up. Another was that the Motown "sound," successful for over a decade, was being challenged by a new Philadelphia "sound" that was more hard-edged and sophisticated and borrowed more freely from white rock 'n roll. In the record world, albums began to replace singles in popularity. But the people who bought albums wanted lots of original songs on them. Motown had always concentrated on singles. Its albums had included lots of "covers," or renditions of songs that had already been recorded and made popular by other artists. Some people say that Berry Gordy was so busy producing movies that he stopped paying as much attention to his record business as he should have. He was then concentrating on *Lady Sings the Blues*, a film biography of the late singer Billie Holiday, starring Diana Ross.

Whatever the reasons for the decline in sales of their records, the Jackson Five, as a group and as individuals, needed something new and different. To Joe Jackson, it seemed the perfect time to let his sons get more involved in writing and producing their own material. They had been writing songs for some time now—Michael and Jermaine especially. Joe Jackson had encouraged them by installing a small recording studio in their home. But the Motown executives turned down the idea. It was not the company's practice to give its artists much creative control. There was some resentment on the part of the Jacksons over this issue. But they were still members-in-good-standing of the Motown family. In December 1973, nineteen-year-old Jermaine married Berry Gordy's daughter Hazel.

Jermaine's marriage had a much greater effect on Michael than Tito's had. Of all the brothers, Jermaine was the one to whom Michael had always felt closest. As a four-year-old he had mimicked Jermaine's singing and eventually won himself a place in the family performing group. He had always idolized his older brother. As the years passed, the age gap had narrowed and they had become best friends. When Jermaine married it meant that he was leaving home, though like Tito he would not move far away. Things would not be the same between him and Michael. For the first time, Michael began to understand that life and relationships did change.

Perhaps Joe Jackson was affected by Jermaine's marriage, too. He saw his boys going their separate ways and wanted to stress the *family*. Since he hadn't gotten anywhere with Motown on the issue of more creative control, he pushed for more influence over their onstage performances. When the Jackson Five were invited to perform in Las Vegas for the first time, he insisted on deciding who would perform and how. For their engagement at the huge new MGM Grand Hotel, he brought the family together as they had been when they were first starting out. The act included all the Jackson children, including Maureen, who had married and moved to Kentucky some years before, LaToya, and Janet. Katherine Jackson came up with the idea of having the two youngest kids, Randy and seven-year-old Janet, imitate famous show business couples like Sonny and Cher. Michael planned choreography that would include the new members of the act.

By this time, Michael had become a very talented choreographer. His own dancing was one of the most exciting parts of the Jackson Five's onstage performance. He had always been a natural dancer, and his talent at mimicry had enabled him to copy the movements of singer James Brown almost exactly. When the people at Motown had told him he should come up with a style of his own, Michael took that advice seriously. But he still looked to other dancers for inspiration. The surprising thing is that his new idol was a much older, white performer—Fred Astaire. Michael loved old movies, and his favorites were from the 1940s, more than ten years before he was even born. Astaire made many movies featuring his dancing, and Michael got video cassettes of those movies and studied them for hours. He used many of the ideas he got from those movies in his own act and in the choreographing he did for his family.

In Las Vegas, their audiences, which were made up mostly of middle-aged people from the Midwest, liked the family act. The Jacksons later went on tour with the show.

The success of the show caused Joe Jackson to feel that the family could get along without Motown. Their records still were not selling very well. They had one hit in 1974 with their disco-beat single "Dancing Machine." But the album that followed it was again mostly "filler." Joe Jackson believed that it might have been a hit if his sons had been allowed to write some of the songs and help produce the album. Resentments between the Jackson family and Motown continued to grow, although both sides tried hard not to let the feelings explode. Everyone was trying not to make the situation hard for Jermaine Jackson and Hazel Gordy Jackson.

But as the months wore on, it became clear that something had to be done. The Jacksons felt increasingly stifled by the Motown formula and by Motown's continued refusal to let them sing the songs they had written. All the boys were writing songs by this time, but Motown did not take their efforts seriously. The Jacksons' resentment over this issue reminded them of other things about Motown that they did not like. As Michael later explained, "At Motown we wanted to do our own writing, but that wasn't in our contract and they wouldn't give it to us. We didn't have publishing rights either, and we had trouble getting a proper accounting of our money. . . . Producers were an issue, too. For the *Dancing Machine* album we were forced to use several producers when we only wanted one producer for the entire album, so it would have one sound. Instead we had a bunch of different sounds, and it wasn't as good as it could have been."

They felt the same way about the records Motown released in 1975. None of them sold well enough to make the top of the charts, and that included Michael's two solo albums, *Forever, Michael* and *The Best of Michael Jackson*, and two singles, "We're Almost There" and "Just a Little Bit of You."

Money is always a big issue in any business. At Motown it was often a bigger issue than at other record companies. One reason was that the company was very secretive about its finances. None of its gold or platinum records was actually "certified" until about 1980-1981 because Motown would not open its account books for outside inspection until that time. Motown also had a curious practice that most record companies did not share. Its artists always recorded many more songs than were ever released. Motown people chose only the best recordings from among them. Yet, Motown charged the expenses for doing all the recordings against the artists' royalties. Thus, the Jackson Five had to pay for studio time and musicians' salaries for fifteen recordings when only five were ever issued. If those five recordings were big hits, then the artists like the Jackson Five were not likely to complain. But when the money stopped rolling in, they started looking more carefully at the way such things were handled.

Quite a few artists had left Motown and signed with other labels. They included Gladys Knight and the Pips and the Temptations. In the summer of 1975 Joe Jackson announced that when their current contract with Motown expired in eight months, they too would leave the label and go with Epic Records.

It was a big step, and in the end it meant the loss of Jermaine. He had to make the difficult choice between following his father and brothers or staying with his wife and father-in-law. His father wanted him to sign with Epic, but he chose to stay with Motown. For a long time after that, his father would not speak to him, and his relationship with the rest of the family was strained. He performed with his family for the last time in Las Vegas later that summer. Michael would say, "Ever since we started singing, Jermaine was in a certain spot near me onstage. All of a sudden he was gone. It felt bare on that side for a long time."

4

$\mathcal{T}$he Jackson Five Become The Jacksons

Joe Jackson signed formally with Epic Records in the spring of 1976, but the Jacksons were not really free of Berry Gordy's company until 1980. That's when all the lawsuits were finally settled. Motown insisted on keeping all rights to the name the Jackson Five, and to all material recorded by all Jacksons while the family was under contract to the company. For years afterward, Motown released albums by the Jackson Five, often just a little while after Epic issued an album by the group. This didn't bother the Jacksons as much as the loss of their name. They had been the Jackson Five for so long that they felt empty, just as the place onstage where Jermaine had always been felt empty for a long time. But Motown had a good case for keeping rights to the name and eventually won most of the lawsuits. The Jackson Five could no longer be the Jackson Five. The new group name they chose was The Jacksons.

As for Jermaine, Motown rewarded him for his loyalty by issuing his solo albums at the rate of about one a year from the time the rest of his family signed with Epic. *My Name Is Jermaine,* his first album after the rest of the family left Motown, was released in late 1976, around the same time as his brothers' first album for Epic.

By the terms of their contract with Epic, The Jacksons enjoyed a higher royalty rate on their records, the opportunity to have their own publishing company, and more control over the material they recorded. They also got the chance to record some of the songs they had written. Two of their compositions were on the first album they recorded for Epic, *The Jacksons.* One was Michael's "Blues Away" and the other was "Style of Life," written by Michael and Tito. The album went gold, as did "Enjoy Yourself," another single from that album. The success of both the album and the single caused the family to feel that they had indeed been right to leave Motown. The fact that critics did not think much of these recordings did not bother them very much, and it seemed to have little effect on their record sales. Nor did it cause any slowdown in the number of personal appearances they were invited to make or on the size of their audience. Joe Jackson and the executives at Epic worked hard to see that The Jacksons were highly "exposed" during their first months with their new label. Not only did they perform at many concerts and make guest appearances on TV shows, but also they had a summer TV series of their own that was such a hit that they returned the following summer.

During the first three years after The Jacksons signed with Epic they took great pains to be very democratic about their music and their performing. They shared lead vocals much more than they had done at Motown. Joe Jackson may have had

While filming *The Wiz* in New York in 1977, Michael had his own apartment and went to parties at the famous Studio 54. But there were a lot of experiences he had to miss because he was so famous.

something to do with this, for he was intent on stressing The Jacksons as a family. But another reason may have been that Michael was not able to sing lead as he had once done. His voice changed. In the normal teenage transition, his voice was deepening and he no longer had complete control over it. He was leaving boyhood behind and becoming a man. He turned eighteen on August 29, 1976, and suddenly he was the "heartthrob" of The Jacksons.

He didn't like this new kind of attention. He had a few dates with Tatum O'Neal, daughter of actor Ryan O'Neal, and an actress in her own right. Fan magazines reported every move they made. Michael did not like seeing his private life made public. Because he was very shy, very slim, and had a very high voice even though it was deepening a little, the rumor got started that he was homosexual. He became even more wary of reporters and interviews.

Faced with mobs of girls making him feel like spaghetti, reports that he liked boys more than girls, beset by reporters and photographers whenever he ventured out, Michael retreated into himself. He stayed home most of the time. By now, there were fewer Jacksons at home. Marlon had gotten married in the summer of 1975 and bought his own house. Jackie had married and moved out the year before that. Michael and Randy were the only Jackson boys left at home. For Michael, the house in Encino became a haven from the outside world. The only times he went out, except for occasional dates, were to perform or record with his brothers. He could not even go to the store without being mobbed by fans and seeing his every move reported in the papers. "I may want to go walking or sit in a tree, but everything we do is on TV or in the newspapers," he said. He had to channel his energies into his music.

The Jacksons made a second album, *Goin' Places*, for Epic in 1977. The same producers worked on it as on the earlier Epic album, and like the first album for that label it included two songs written by the Jacksons: "Different Kind of Lady" and "Do What You Wanna." They also produced these two tracks. But it was not as big a hit as their first album, and Joe Jackson used this as one of his arguments in favor of giving his sons even greater say in their recordings. He wanted them to do more writing and producing.

But before the group recorded their next album for Epic, Michael got a chance to work in another creative field, the movie business. He was cast as the scarecrow in the movie version of *The Wiz*.

The Wiz was a black, urban version of *The Wizard of Oz*. It had opened as a Broadway musical in 1975, had been that year's big Tony Award winner, and ran for nearly four years. The idea for a movie version of *The Wiz* was conceived not long after the Broadway show became a hit. By 1977 all the parts were cast, and rehearsals began in New York in mid-summer. Diana Ross would play Dorothy, Richard Pryor the Wiz, Lena Horne the good witch Glinda.

When Michael was offered the part of the Scarecrow, he jumped at the chance. He had wanted to be in a movie ever since he had spent time on the set of *Lady Sings the Blues* with Diana Ross back in 1971-1972. To him, it was even better that his first movie part would be in a film starring Diana Ross.

He almost lost the chance to play the role. On July 4, 1977, just days before principal filming began, Michael suffered an attack of pneumothorax. Bubbles had formed in his lungs, and when they burst he couldn't breathe. No one knew exactly why it had happened. Usually, pneumothorax strikes people who

smoke. Michael had never smoked—either regular cigarettes or marijuana. He had been offered marijuana but had always refused it. In fact, he didn't even like the word "high." He was very thin, weighing only about 115 pounds, so there was not much fat around his lungs to protect them. Perhaps his singing all the time had proven too much for his lungs. Although he had to be hospitalized and was advised to rest after he left the hospital, Michael refused to give up his role in *The Wiz*. When principal photography began, he was there.

He moved into a high-rise apartment in New York. He had just turned nineteen, and it was the first time he had ever been on his own. He brought along his video cassettes of Fred Astaire musicals and his music magazines. He could spend hours alone with them. For company, he could count on Diana Ross. His parents and brothers visited often. Friends his own age? He really didn't have any to miss. As he told Penelope Ross of *Viva* Magazine, "I'm around grownups all the time. The only chance I get to see kids is at concerts when they're screaming."

He did make one friend who was around his own age while he was in New York—Stephanie Mills. She was the star of *The Wiz* on Broadway, and Michael went to see that show about fifteen times. Taken backstage and introduced to Stephanie, he was as excited as one of his own fans would have been at meeting him. The two talked on the telephone all the time and were seen together enough to start a whole new round of gossip about Michael Jackson's love life. Because he could not enjoy much privacy, even in New York, Michael did not get to see much else on Broadway besides *The Wiz*.

There were a lot of experiences he had to miss because he was so famous. His protected existence denied him knowledge of some very basic things. In the fall of 1978, an interviewer for *Crawdaddy* arranged to meet him in a French restaurant in midtown Manhattan. Michael arrived with two publicists from Epic, but he still felt unsure of himself. "I don't always feel right in these places. I don't know how everything works," he told the interviewer. Wrote the interviewer, "His own professional singlemindedness has imposed a marked distance between Jackson and the outside world."

Michael was aware of that distance. As he explained to Charles L. Sanders of *Ebony* in 1979, "My brothers say that *everybody* intimidates me. That's not true, but I do avoid eye contact with a lot of people. I'd much rather talk on the phone."

Michael spent most of his time in New York doing the best job he could in the role of the Scarecrow in the movie version of *The Wiz*. The work was a lot harder than he had expected it to be. He had to spend four hours a day for five months getting made up. His wig was made of steel wool pads, a peanut butter cup covered his nose. Layers and layers of pancake makeup covered his face. As the months wore on, the weather grew cold, but the cast still worked outside a great deal and tried not to think about how uncomfortable they were. Michael studied his lines, tried different movements and gestures. He wanted to *become* the Scarecrow. He concentrated so hard in fact that in some ways he *did* become the Scarecrow. There were times when he would not want to take off his costume and makeup at the end of the day. When asked once how it felt to be an actor, he said that he considered himself not so much an actor as a "believer."

The Wiz movie was released in 1978. It did not get very good reviews. Film critics said that it was too lavish and too expensive. They said that Diana Ross, at age thirty-four, just wasn't believable as the teenage Dorothy. But they had good things to say about Michael. All his hard work paid off, for his Scarecrow character was believable. Being part of that movie was a valuable experience for him. It also introduced him to Quincy Jones, who served as musical director on the film. Out of that meeting would come one of the most successful collaborations in the history of music.

Not long after he completed principal filming on *The Wiz*, Michael went back into the Epic recording studios with his brothers. For their third album with the label, *Destiny*, The Jacksons got the chance to produce all the tracks themselves, although two people from CBS, which owned the label, oversaw their work as executive producers.

Destiny was a "concept" album, built around the idea of brotherhood, not the kind among brothers but the kind among people. Michael chose a peacock for the back of the album cover because it had all colors in its tail. He had read about peacocks in a magazine and felt that the bird was a fine symbol for brotherhood. His family liked the idea of the peacock symbol, and they decided to name their production company

With Diana Ross and Nipsey Russell (the Tin Man) in *The Wiz*. Michael became so deeply involved in his Scarecrow character that at the end of a day's shooting he didn't want to take off his costume and makeup.

Peacock Productions. *Destiny* was released in the fall of 1978 and went platinum, their first album to sell over a million copies. Michael and Randy's song, "Shake Your Body (Down to the Ground)" was released as a single early in 1979. It, too, went platinum and was their first platinum single in five years.

The year 1979 marked The Jackson's tenth year as major recording artists. Their first album, *Diana Ross Presents the Jackson Five*, had been issued in 1969. To celebrate the event, The Jacksons went on a "world tour" that began January 22 in Bremen, Germany; continued in Madrid, Spain; Amsterdam,

Holland; Geneva, Switzerland; Paris, France; and twelve cities in England, and ended in the African capital of Nairobi, Kenya. In each city, Michael looked for children. Sometimes he was saddened by what he saw, as in Africa, where children were suffering from malnutrition and were living in flimsy shacks. But overall he was thrilled to see so many different kinds of people. He has said, "By traveling the world, I know there must be a God. I've seen so much. I've been in the poorest of homes and the richest of homes. Sometimes I just want to take all the children of the world in my arms. . . really!"

At age twenty, Michael Jackson was in the unique position of knowing more about the capitals of Europe than he did about downtown Encino. He was developing a world view. He understood that he was different from all but a handful of other people his age. He realized that there were very few human beings on earth who would ever have the fame and the money he had. Sometimes, it was a little scary to think about. "Why me?" he would ask himself. The only answer that seemed to make any sense to him was that he had been chosen by God. If he had been chosen, then God must have had a special purpose. To find out what the purpose could be, Michael began to study the Bible and devote more time to the Jehovah's Witnesses. He was eventually baptized as a Witness, the only Jackson child besides Maureen to do so. While he found no easy answers, somehow religion gave him the patience to keep searching.

In the meantime, Michael was eager to express his ideas and display his musical gifts. He had not recorded a solo album since 1975. Partly, that was because his voice had changed. But partly, too, it was because of the change from Motown to Epic and his father's desire that the Jacksons stress the group and not individuals. By the time Michael told his father that he wanted to do

During a visit to London in 1979, Michael posed for publicity pictures in a Charlie Chaplin costume. His stage idols are people from the past, and his favorite movies are 1940s musicals.

an album by himself, Joe Jackson believed that The Jacksons had survived the switch of record labels and their change of name. Besides, at twenty, Michael had a right to make his own decisions.

With his father and the executives at Epic willing to go along with his wishes, Michael set about finding a producer for his album. Although he'd had some experience producing, he knew he wasn't ready to produce a whole album, and certainly not his own. Nor were the people at Epic ready to finance such a venture. Michael called Quincy Jones, who had been musical director on *The Wiz*, and asked him to recommend some producers. He was delighted when Jones offered to produce the album.

Quincy Jones was a thirty-year veteran of the music business. He had worked with Billie Holiday, Frank Sinatra, Leslie Gore, and many other artists. In the 1960s he had been one of the few blacks writing film soundtracks and had been nominated for an Academy Award for his film work. Michael could not have asked for a better man to produce his album, and he probably had hoped to work with Jones when he asked Jones to recommend someone else. The two met to discuss Michael's album and found that they shared a lot of the same musical ideas. Michael's ideas about his album were still unformed. His main wish was that it have a completely different sound from the Epic recordings by The Jacksons. Jones helped him to define his ideas.

Together they chose the material for the album. It would include three songs Michael had written—"Don't Stop 'Til You Get Enough," "Working Day and Night," and, with a man named Louis Johnson, "Get On The Floor." They also chose a song written by Stevie Wonder and former Supreme Susaye Greene called "I Can't Help It" and a song written by Carol Bayer Sager and David Foster called "It's Like Falling in Love."

Former Beatle Paul McCartney and his wife Linda invited Michael to their house and gave him a song they had written for him called "Girlfriend." He and Quincy Jones decided to include it on the album. Among the other songs were "She's Out of My Life" by Tom Bahler and three by Rod Temperton: "Rock With You," "Burn This Disco Out," and "Off The Wall," which was chosen as the album's title.

Michael and Quincy Jones decided how to present each song—which instrumental background, what kind of beat. They wanted most of the numbers to be danceable. They chose backup singers for choruses. Once they had decided on how to do a song, Michael went home and practiced. That pleased Quincy, for he had worked with some singers who arrived at the recording studio "cold."

Michael did a lot more than just practice. He was involved in every stage of production. The way recordings are made, the instrumental tracks are laid down first, each instrument on a separate track so it is easy to replace or rework them later. Then the singer goes into the studio, puts on a headset, listens to the instrumental portion of the song, and sings along with it. Michael was at the studio during the instrumental recording stage, and he would either take the tapes home or have them sent there by messenger. Because he had a recording studio at home, he could listen to the instrumental tracks and practice singing, tape the result, and decide what worked and what didn't.

With Michael so well prepared, the actual in-studio recording of most of the songs did not take long. But with "She's Out of My Life," Quincy Jones wondered if he was ever going to get a recording that didn't include Michael's sobs. The song is a ballad about lost love, and it obviously struck a deep chord in Michael. Jones later said, "I'd look up at the end, and Michael would be crying. I said, 'We'll come back in two weeks and do it again, and maybe it won't tear you up so much.' We came back and he started to get teary. . . so we left it in." As the weeks passed, Michael and Quincy became close, and Quincy, whom everyone calls "Q," started calling Michael by a nickname. It is "Smelly." Just as Michael doesn't like the word "high," he does not like the word "funky." He says "smelly" instead. Jones thought that was funny.

Once both instrumental and vocal tracks for a song had been laid down, the next step was the "mixing." Jones and the engineer adjusted each track for loudness, vocal pitch, the amount of treble or bass on each instrument. Michael was thoroughly involved in this process, too, making suggestions about adding more backup voices, or softening a particular instrument at a certain point. He listened to the final master tape, and checked the test pressing for quality. Meanwhile, he was helping to decide on the album cover and the kind of advertising that would be done to promote it. He was in on every step, and when *Off The Wall* was finished he was proud not just of the way he sang the songs but of the entire product. He listened to it over and over again, and liked it better each time. Quincy Jones liked it, too, and they were both sure that it would be a hit. They just didn't know how big a hit.

Off The Wall was released in the spring of 1979, and it was a smash—more successful than Michael or Quincy had ever dreamed. It quickly climbed into the Top Ten on the album charts and stayed there for nearly eight months. During that time it sold over seven million copies. The Jacksons' most recent album, *Destiny*, had sold more than one million copies and been certified platinum, the highest recognition for an album. By contrast, Michael's album was platinum seven times! And it didn't go platinum just in the United States but in Britain, Australia, and Canada as well.

That wasn't all. In July 1979, Epic began to release selected tracks from the album as single records. "Don't Stop 'Til You Get Enough" was the first. It became Number One in the country and was certified platinum. "Rock With You" came out a couple of months later and "Off The Wall," the album's title track, a few months after that. Both made the Top Ten and went gold. When "She's Out of My Life," released in early 1980, also made the Top Ten and sold more than a million copies, Michael Jackson made history: His was the first solo record album ever to produce four Top Ten hits. (In England, a fifth single, Paul and Linda McCartney's "Girlfriend," was issued, and *Off The Wall* became the first album to produce five hit singles in that country.)

In the early part of 1980, the awards began to pour in. At the American Music Awards ceremony in January, Michael tied Donna Summer for the most awards. The three he won, all in the Soul category, were Favorite Male Vocalist, Favorite Album, and Favorite Single for "Don't Stop 'Til You Get Enough." Two months later he won a Grammy Award for Best Rhythm and Blues Vocal Performance for "Don't Stop 'Til You Get Enough."

Clearly, Michael Jackson was a candidate to be the superstar of the new decade of the 1980s. But to claim that title he would have to leave The Jacksons and go out on his own. He wasn't quite ready to do that. He was glad he had been able to show what he could do, but he also felt that he should continue recording and appearing with his brothers. He could not turn his back on his father's vision of the family—being individuals but staying together. That vision had worked for the Jacksons for a long time. LaToya Jackson recorded and released her first album that year. Issued by the Polydor label, it contained a song written by LaToya and Michael and produced by Michael, "Night Time Lover." And Michael was fully involved with his brothers in the writing, producing, and recording of their fourth album for Epic, *Triumph*.

Triumph, released in 1980, contained six songs written by The Jacksons, one written by Michael and Jackie, one written by Michael, and one written by Jackie. Four of the songs became hits as singles, and the album itself went platinum. To publicize the album and to take advantage of the "Jacksonmania" that both The Jacksons and Michael alone had started, The Jacksons went on a thirty-city national tour in 1981. The tour was a family venture. Michael himself was not eager to do it. When the family agreed to let him have primary control over the show, he allowed himself to be talked into it for their sake.

The show was largely created by Michael, with an electronic space-age set, lots of magical illusions created by magician Doug Henning, and exciting choreography. Each concert opened with a videotape made under Michael's supervision, set to the music of "Can You Feel It," and full of wonderful fantasy images. In one sequence, The Jacksons were giants lifting a rainbow and causing stardust to fall on the cities of the earth. Children of all races were bathed in the rainbow's colors and reached out to take each other's hands. In another, The Jacksons, each encased in his own bubble, drifted down to earth.

Randy, who was now twenty-one, had been in a serious automobile accident four years before, in 1977. He had suffered temporary paralysis and had been advised at first by doctors that he might never be able to walk again. His total recovery had been nothing short of miraculous, and to make this point Randy

Michael and Diana Ross at the 1981 American Music Awards. Michael's first solo album, *Off The Wall*, was named Favorite Soul Album.

opened each show wearing a suit of armor and leading his brothers onto the stage.

The tour included two performances in Atlanta, Georgia. At that time, Atlanta's black community was living in terror, for a killer of young children was on the loose. More than twenty youngsters had disappeared or been found murdered. At Michael's request, most of the profits from the two shows went to help find Atlanta's missing children. Michael still had a special love of children, and often said that children were smarter than grownups.

In many ways, Michael at twenty-two was still a child himself. He had the innocence of a child. He had been in Hollywood for years but acted like the kid next door. Back in 1979 he had spent a month in New England with the cast and crew of the movie *On Golden Pond*. He talked for hours with Jane Fonda, her father Henry Fonda, and Katharine Hepburn. He was so excited about the things these people had to say that he tape-recorded their conversations! To Michael, that was a perfectly logical thing to do. He knew he couldn't remember everything that was said. But most twenty-two-year-olds would have been afraid to admit that anything said by people who were over forty (Henry Fonda and Katharine Hepburn were over sixty-five!) was worth taping.

But in other ways Michael was wise beyond his years. All that stuff about children and animals and no drugs and a world that was beautiful didn't keep Michael from wanting to know exactly how much money he had and how many of his records were being sold. Quincy Jones was amazed to learn that Michael knew not only how much money (royalty) he earned from the sale of each record in the United States, but also everywhere else, for the royalty rates differed from country to country. Michael had his own accountants and lawyers to handle the money from his records and his share earned from the Jacksons' records and tours. He did not just put it all into the family "till."

When The Jacksons' 1981 tour ended, he took another step toward independence. He announced that the tour was his last. "I love being on stage, but I don't like the other things that go with touring," he told Robert Hilburn of the *Los Angeles Times*. He didn't like staying in hotels, the scheduling worries, the constant moving from one place to another. It is possible, too, that he was tired of trying to fit himself into a group that he had outgrown. He wanted to do another solo album. He wanted to do more film work. He could not have the freedom to do these things as a member of The Jacksons.

There was no "official split." Michael never announced that he was leaving The Jacksons, although newspaper reporters and gossip columnists ran stories to that effect. He stayed with Epic Records and remained at home in Encino. But *The Jacksons Live*, the two-record, live album that resulted from the 1981 tour, was the last recording he did with his brothers until 1984.

Meanwhile, another split was taking place in the Jackson family. Although it was not widely reported, Joe and Katherine Jackson separated, and in 1982 they quietly began divorce proceedings.

5

$\mathcal{M}$ichael Jackson

Along with his decision to become independent of his brothers as a performer, Michael Jackson decided to change his "look." For onstage performing, he started wearing sequined jackets and socks and short pants. He also began to wear one white glove on his right hand. At first he wore the single glove only when he was performing, but soon he wore it whenever he was in the public spotlight, such as at awards ceremonies. Some people believed that the glove stood for purity. But Michael insisted that it stood for his role as an entertainer. When he wore it, he was "on," and as long as he did wear it, he was able to deal with the outside world. For public appearances he also took to wearing sequined military jackets, along with the white glove. He also wore dark glasses as a kind of shield.

At home, in private, he dressed any old way. But there was another part of his "look" that he changed that he could not take off and put on. Michael Jackson had plastic surgery to make his nose thinner. Some people think he also had his eyes widened and his cheekbones raised, but his mother insisted to a reporter for *Time* magazine in 1984 that the only thing that was changed was his nose. Michael will not talk about why he had cosmetic surgery. Some people believe that he wanted to look like Diana Ross. Indeed, they do look very much like each other now. Michael idolizes Diana. In fact, he has said he would like to marry her. Given the difference in their ages, and the fact that she thinks of Michael as a son, that is not likely to happen. But Michael can look as much like her as possible and be closer to her in that way.

Michael began the year 1982 by writing a song for Diana Ross. Titled "Muscles," the name of Michael's snake, it was a very sexy song, and Diana really liked it. In fact, she suggested that Michael produce the record for her. But Michael just could not see himself doing that. He wasn't sure that he had enough experience. He suggested that they produce it together. But Diana stood firm. She wanted Michael to take full responsibility. At last he agreed. The record became a big hit for Diana, her first in a long time. The young man whom she liked to call her "baby" had truly grown up.

Michael's next project was the recording of two duets with Paul McCartney. Both "Say, Say, Say" and "The Man" were on McCartney's new album. In return, Michael asked McCartney to record a duet for *his* next album, and McCartney agreed. Michael was already planning his second solo album for Epic. There was no question in his mind that Quincy Jones would produce it, but this time Michael wanted to act as co-producer.

The two followed the same steps as they had for *Off The Wall*. First, they selected material. Once again Rod Temperton wrote the title track, "Thriller," as well as "The Lady in My Life"

Michael in 1984. The sequined jacket and single white glove had become his trademarks.

and "Baby Be Mine." Michael contributed three songs—"Beat It," "Billie Jean," and "Wanna Be Startin' Somethin'." He and Paul McCartney wrote the song they sang together, "The Girl Is Mine." It was a musical "first," for although it was the old story of two men competing for the same girl, the two men in this case were of different races. Even Quincy Jones wrote a song, "PYT (Pretty Young Thing)," and it was recorded with Michael's sisters Janet and LaToya singing backup.

Michael asked other well-known artists to contribute to the album. White rock guitarist Eddie Van Halen played on "Beat It." The rock group Toto played backup on several cuts. This kind of collaboration among name artists was happening more and more often, and Michael's *Thriller* album was an example of how successful it could be. The album was full of energy and creativity, and it was marked by the same careful attention to production as was *Off The Wall*.

Again, Michael was present in the recording studio during the laying down of instrumental tracks, the overdubbing, and mixing. This time the "sound" of the final cuts was even denser—there were more tracks, more to hear, a greater variety of sound. One could listen to a track from the album over and over and each time hear something new. Again, Michael practiced singing along with the instrumental tracks until he had just the right sound.

As soon as *Thriller* was released in late 1982, it began to sell at a brisk pace. Not only was it popular among fans of Michael Jackson, but it received excellent reviews from music critics who were less interested in Michael as a personality than as a musician. Here are some of the things that Mitchell Cohen, the reviewer for *High Fidelity* magazine, had to say: "*Thriller* is a sleek and sharp machine, a work of amazing confidence and pacing . . . . On the surface, the LP just zips along like a variety

Michael with Paul McCartney. "The Girl Is Mine," the song they wrote and recorded together for Michael's *Thriller* album, was a musical first.

———————

show, complete with guest stars, production numbers, dance tunes . . . . It's rare to hear commercial pop music makers who have such a definite sense of what they're up to, who don't just touch all the bases, but breeze around them with flair, tipping their hats to the bleachers as they go. Michael Jackson and Quincy Jones are genuine crowd-pleasers." People who wanted to categorize *Thriller* were calling it pop-soul.

Early on, Michael was pretty sure that *Thriller* would sell as well as *Off The Wall*, if not better. He also looked forward to the release of selected tracks from the album as singles.

It takes a lot of time and work to produce a record album, and if Michael had decided to take some time to rest after finishing *Thriller*, that rest would have been well deserved. But Michael didn't rest. He plunged immediately into another project, his first recorded narration.

The movie *E.T.—The Extra-Terrestrial* had been released at the start of the summer and was an immediate hit. In months there were E.T. dolls, lunch boxes, games, T-shirts, coloring books, and all sorts of other things. The movie's sound track was released as an instrumental album. As time went on, though, Steven Spielberg, the director of the movie and the creator of E.T., decided that there should also be a storybook album. He talked to Michael and Quincy Jones about it. Michael loved the idea. MCA Records would issue the album, and that company got a release from Epic Records so Michael could do it. Michael narrated the story, and for him one of the best parts of the whole experience was meeting E.T. "He grabbed me," Michael later recalled. "He put his arms around me. He was so real that I was talking to him." He told Charles L. Sanders of *Ebony* magazine, "When I was doing that recording I really felt that I was E.T., and it was because his story is the story of my life in many ways." During the part where E.T. seems to be dying, Michael cried, and Quincy Jones left the crying in, just as he had on "She's Out Of My Life."

Michael also sang a beautiful ballad written by Rod Temperton called "Someone in the Dark." The record contained dialogue from the film. It was the finest storybook album ever produced, and the people at MCA planned a lot of promotion. They even pressed a single of the song "Someone in the Dark."

The trouble was, MCA issued the storybook album and the single at the end of 1982, the same time that Epic Records issued the *Thriller* album. CBS Records, owner of the Epic label, was afraid that the single "Someone in the Dark" would interfere with the sales of *Thriller*. CBS took the case to court and got the single taken off the market. Michael liked the song and was sorry that the record could not be sold. But he had a very keen understanding of the record business and knew that it was bigger than any individual song or artist. Besides, he was soon caught up in the amazing story of *Thriller*. His second solo album for Epic quickly became a phenomenon—a record the likes of which had never been seen before.

Within two weeks after its release, *Thriller* was Number 11 on the album charts. By the next week it was Number 9. By early March 1983 it was Number One. Meanwhile, the first single from the album, the title song "Thriller," was released. The week of January 22, 1983, the second single, "Billie Jean," came out. Three weeks later, it was the Number One song in the country.

Written by Michael, it is a song about a paternity suit: A girl named Billie Jean has accused Michael of fathering her baby. In real life, Michael had recently faced a paternity suit, and that was probably his inspiration for the song. The lyrics, or the story the song tells, are not as important as the hiccupping, driving beat. You can't listen to it and remain still. The key to the rhythm is its drums. Drummer Ndugu Chanceler once explained how that driving instrumental background came about: "Michael always knew how he wanted it to sound. There was originally just a drum machine track on it. I came in and cut a live drum track over the overdub, so that at times during the record there is just me and then the two together." That is the kind of "density" that is on the tracks of *Thriller*. You can listen to it over and over again and each time hear more of what is being done with the drum tracks.

"Beat It," the third single, was released the week of March 5, 1983. It was a song about gang warfare, something Michael did not personally know anything about. He had read about wars between street gangs in Los Angeles, though. Again, the lyrics are not as important as the sound. It had a drive and an energy due to the counterpoint between Michael's voice and the heavy-metal guitar of Eddie Van Halen. "Beat It" soon reached Number One on the popular charts. But what was especially important was that it also received play on radio stations that did not ordinarily play records by blacks.

Believe it or not, there is still quite a bit of racial segregation in the music industry. It comes from radio and music-television station managers more than from the artists or the audiences. Over the last ten years, radio stations have tended to "specialize": Some are all talk and no music, others are all music and no talk. The all-music stations are specialized: country-western, jazz, easy-listening, classical, soul, AOR (Album Oriented Rock). There is a station in New York that plays nothing but love songs. Until "Beat It" was released, most rock stations did not feature black artists very often. But because of the guitar track provided by Eddie Van Halen, the rock stations played "Beat It." Even without the guitar playing of Eddie Van Halen, the song probably would have reached the rock airwaves. It simply appealed to practically everybody. Wrote Wayne Robbins in *Newsday*, July 10, 1983, "The Jackson album is having a profound effect on the music industry for reasons that have nothing to do with aesthetics. *Thriller* has transcended the boundaries that have made the music industry increasingly segregated over the last ten years. . . a decade during which the black music industry and the white rock industry grew along parallel lines." This was just one of the breakthroughs Michael made with *Thriller*. Another had to do with the integration of music video TV stations.

Music video was a brand new industry. It had started in 1979, the same year that Michael's earlier Epic album *Off The Wall* was released. MTV, the major music video channel, did not go on the air until 1981. When he was putting together *Thriller*, Michael kept in mind the idea of doing music videos of some of the tracks, and he went to work on that idea when he finished the album.

He had done his homework. He had talked with Paul McCartney about the way the Beatles had made movies like *A Hard Day's Night*, which was basically a film showing the group performing their songs in various odd locations. He had studied the latest music videos by rock artists and studied the work of directors who had worked on videos. He thought about the various tracks on his album and about which ones could best be translated to video. Then he went to work.

He hired director Steve Barron, and with the people at Epic they decided to do a video of "Billie Jean." On the face of it, the song would seem to present problems because, after all, it was about a paternity suit. But the video is mostly about Michael being followed by a private detective. Here is how Tom Carson of the *Village Voice* described the *Billie Jean* video: "On a rainy, empty, stylized city street, a private eye tails a figure [Jackson], whose otherworldly aura is signaled by a human light-show: everything he touches briefly glows an eerie, lovely white. When the detective comes upon Jackson in front of a store, every camera in the window goes off, but their pictures only show the private eye reaching for empty air. Finally, we see the reason for the pursuit: Jackson climbs a rickety set of stairs outside a hotel and comes to a room where he looks down on a woman asleep in bed. He climbs in beside her, but when the detective outside tries to photograph them,

Michael at the "Celebrate Michael" party at the Museum of Natural History in New York in February 1984. *Thriller* had made music history for number of copies sold and for the number of hit singles from one album.

the sheet glows and gently collapses where Jackson was lying, [and] the policemen come to take his bewildered tormentor away. As they leave the street, a set of flagstones on the sidewalk gleams in rapid sequence: Jackson, invisibly taking his leave."

In the video, Michael wore a sequined jacket, short pants, white socks, black shoes, and one white glove on his right hand. The way he walked along the city street, creating a square of light with each step, reminded a lot of people of the yellow brick road in *The Wiz*. When he danced, he made jerky motions that went perfectly with the hiccupping beat of the song. In spite of the fact that the video didn't have much to do with the lyrics of the song, it was one of the most exciting videos ever made. There was no way that MTV could *not* play it.

Like the AOR radio stations, the young MTV was rock oriented and showed almost exclusively white videos. Among black artists only Tina Turner had managed to get a video on MTV, and her video was not shown very often. Michael's *Billie Jean* video was the first one by a black artist to be played as often as videos by white artists. That was in March 1983. The following month Michael hit the MTV airwaves with a video that was even more exciting.

His *Beat It* video was directed by Bob Giraldi, who spent endless hours on the telephone with Michael talking about how it should be done. It is a very realistic story about a rivalry between two tough urban gangs, and Michael and Giraldi decided to use real gangs in the video. The unrealistic part is that a skinny kid (Michael) gets the gangs to make peace through dancing. The choreography is like a Broadway production number, like *West Side Story*.

Much of the exciting choreography was the work of Michael Peters, a dancer and choreographer who played the part of one of the gang leaders in the *Beat It* video. Vince Patterson, also a professional dancer, who played the rival gang leader in the video, described Peters' movement as like "cutting through the air without disturbing any molecules." For the *Beat It* video, Peters came up with a brand new step called the Worm. It is an undulating, wave-like step done as you back up. It has since been copied by other choreographers. Michael was so impressed that he decided to have Peters choreograph his next video.

MTV played both of Michael's videos over and over, and its audience didn't complain. MTV had said that its audience was only interested in rock and new-music videos. When the audience proved very interested in Michael Jackson's videos, the way was opened for videos by more black performers. Pretty soon MTV was showing videos by Prince, Sylvester, Bob Marley, and others.

Every month in early 1983 seemed to bring a new break-through by Michael Jackson. In May he made a lot of people in America who didn't know a thing about music sit up and take notice. Motown celebrated its 25th anniversary with a star-studded television special. All the acts that had made Motown famous gathered to do the show—The Temptations, Smokey Robinson, Diana Ross, Stevie Wonder. Motown wanted Michael to be on the special, too, and he agreed. But he insisted on performing "Billie Jean." The Motown people let him do so, and Michael was the only artist on the show who performed a song that had not been produced by Motown.

Millions of people watched the Motown special. It was the highest rated program of that week. People in their forties re-membered buying and dancing to Motown records. People in their early teens were still doing that. It was a nice show, full of music and memories. Film clips showed the artists as they were back in their early Motown days. When the time came to show Motown in the late 1960s-early 1970s, there was a film clip of the Jackson Five and a little kid named Michael singing and dancing his heart out. Then the big screen went dark, and the Michael Jackson of 1983 took the stage. He did "Billie Jean," dancing with that puppet-like, wired energy, wearing his short pants and single glove. Geri Hirshey, writing in *Rolling Stone*, described Michael's movements this way: "He can tuck his long, thin frame into a figure skater's spin without benefit of ice or skates. Aided by the burn and flash of silvery body suits, he seems to change molecular structure at will, all robot angles one second and rippling curves the next." Across the nation, millions of people held their breath, so awed were they by Michael's performance. People who only dimly remembered the Jackson Five suddenly became aware of Michael Jackson. People who missed the Motown 25th Anniversary special when it first aired had the same reaction when it was repeated that fall.

Sales of *Thriller* skyrocketed. People who had not bought an album in years bought *Thriller*. By July it had sold eight million copies. The fourth single from the album, "Wanna Be Startin' Somethin'," had been released by then and quickly rose to Number One on the charts. That made a total of four hit singles from the album. But that was not the end. Two more tracks from the album were released as singles that year—"PYT (Pretty Young Thing)" and "Human Nature." When they, too, were hits, they brought to a total of six the number of hit singles from one album. Considering that there are only nine songs on the album, that is an incredible proportion.

Meanwhile, the album itself had taken possession of the charts. By June 1984 it was still Number 9. And that was just in the United States. *Thriller* wasn't just a national success but a worldwide phenomenon. By late 1983 it had gone platinum in Canada, Great Britain, Holland, Australia, New Zealand, Japan, Germany, France, Sweden, Belgium, Switzerland, Spain, Greece, and South Africa. It had gone gold in Denmark, Italy, Israel, and Norway.

While keeping close track of sales of his album in foreign countries, Michael went to work on a third video. The video for the title track, "Thriller," was like a mini horror film. It was directed by John Landis, who had directed the film *An American Werewolf in London* and one of the segments in the movie *The Twilight Zone*. Landis and Michael had long conversations about what the "Thriller" video would be about. They started with the story of the song: A boy takes a girl to a horror movie and takes advantage of her fear to snuggle up to her. In the video, the people in the audience all turn into monsters. Michael turns into a monster before our eyes! Vincent Price, the king of horror movies, had talked on the *Thriller* album track. He appears in the video as well, giving it even more claim to being a mini horror film.

Michael Peters choreographed the video. His style is to move not according to established dance steps and rhythms but according to the sounds of the instruments. In a way, the body becomes an echo of the instrument, and in a music video that is exciting and new. For Michael Jackson, Michael Peters became a new idol—someone he could work with, not someone he had to watch in 1940s movies.

By the time the *Thriller* video aired in late 1983, the production of videos had become so sophisticated and costly that many people felt they could qualify as short films. Michael Jackson was among them. His video premiered in movie theaters in time to qualify for an Academy Award nomination in the same category with films. While it was some consolation for Michael when he won three awards at the first MTV Video Music Awards in September 1984, he stubbornly held onto his idea that videos were just like movies.

Before the *Thriller* video, videos had been given to MTV, just as records are given to radio stations. The idea is that if videos and records can be played, the public will find out about the records and buy them. It is all a kind of free advertising. But Michael decided that MTV should pay for the *Thriller* video, and his video became the first to be bought by MTV. During the making of the *Thriller* video, cameras recorded the actual process. What resulted was a documentary on the making of the *Thriller* video. Michael sold that to cable TV and to a videocassette manufacturer. No one was about to question Michael's business sense after that.

Next, Michael and Paul McCartney worked together on a video of "Say, Say, Say," which Bob Giraldi, director of the *Beat It* video, directed. Michael loved doing videos. They allowed him to be an actor. They allowed him to dress up in wild costumes and live out his fantasies. They allowed him to *perform* his songs, not just sing them. Best of all, they were something new. For a young man who had been singing professionally since the age of seven and making major recordings since the age of eleven, it was important to have something new to do. Besides, even Michael must have worried sometimes that his album *Thriller* might be untoppable.

As the months wore on, *Thriller* kept making history. It went into the *Guinness Book of World Records* as the all-time best-selling solo record album when it reached sales of 25 million copies worldwide. Not only did it continue to sell at a fantastic rate, but people in the record business gave the album credit for bringing new life to the whole industry. Record sales had not been very good in the early 1980s. The disco craze had died down, and nothing had come along to take its place. When *Thriller* was released, people had to go into record stores to buy it. While they were in the stores they looked around and often bought other records, too. What was good for Michael Jackson also turned out to be good for other recording artists. He was the star of the industry.

At no time was his stardom more evident than during the music awards season in the early months of 1984. First came the American Music Awards in mid-January. Michael, the young male superstar of the 1980s, attended with Brooke Shields, the young female superstar of the 1980s. The two had met at a Hollywood party and had instantly liked one another. When Brooke, who was attending Princeton University in New Jersey, read that Michael had been nominated for a number of American Music Awards, she called to congratulate him. He invited her to attend the awards ceremony at the Houston Astrodome. She flew from Princeton to be with him. That night, they were the most photographed couple in the place, and there were 200,000 people there. Michael won eight awards, including a special Award of Merit. He was the youngest person ever to win that award. People called that awards show The Michael Jackson Show.

The Grammy Awards were next. Twenty-six years old, the awards were like the Oscars of the music business—the most respected prizes for musicians. Michael attended with Brooke Shields again, and also with Emmanuel Lewis, the pint-sized star of the television show *Webster*. They had front-row seats, which was logical, for Michael and his records had been nominated for twelve awards, more than anyone else in the history of the Grammys. It was a pretty sure bet that he would win most of them. As Mickey Rooney, one of the presenters, told the audience, "It's a pleasure doing the Michael Jackson show."

The night did indeed belong to Michael Jackson. He made eight trips up to the podium to accept more awards than any other performer in the history of the Grammys. Each time, he found someone else to thank. He thanked God, of course, his

Michael and Quincy Jones, who produced both *Off The Wall* and *Thriller*, at the 1984 Grammy Awards. Michael won so many of the awards that people called the ceremony "the Michael Jackson show."

family, his producers, the executives at Epic, the girls in the balcony! He even took off his dark glasses once, saying that he had promised Katharine Hepburn he would. He and Hepburn had been friends ever since he had visited the New Hampshire set of *On Golden Pond* in 1979. She had invited him to dinner. He had invited her to be a VIP guest at The Jacksons' concert in New York in 1981, and she had attended—her first rock concert. They talked frequently on the telephone, and Michael didn't see anything strange about having as a friend a woman who was old enough to be his grandmother. Nor did he think it strange to have Emmanuel Lewis as a friend. When he accepted one award, he invited Lewis to join him at the podium. Little

Emmanuel climbed the stairs to the stage as if they were mountain crags. Once he had made it to the podium, Michael lifted him to his shoulder. The audience, and the 60 million people who watched it all on TV, loved every minute of it.

Here is the list of Grammy Awards Michael won that night:

Producer of the Year (with Quincy Jones) for *Thriller*

Album of the Year

Best Male Rhythm-and-Blues Vocal for "Billie Jean"

Best New Rhythm-and-Blues Song for "Billie Jean"

Best Children's Album for *E.T.: The Extra-Terrestrial*

Best Male Pop Vocal for "Thriller"

Best Male Rock Vocal for "Beat It"

Record of the Year for "Beat It"

In winning so many awards, Michael beat out some very tough competition. Some very talented people did not win because Michael did win. Amidst all the celebration and hoopla, Michael remembered that Lionel Richie had been nominated for a lot of Grammys for his album *All Night Long*. Michael made a point of mentioning Lionel Richie and praising him as a person and as a songwriter. That reminded a lot of people that Michael Jackson, superstar, still manages to care about others and to be sensitive to their feelings. And Brooke Shields later reported that even though Michael made eight trips to the podium, he did not become overconfident. She says, "He'd come back and he'd sit down with me and he'd say, 'Was that okay? Did I do all right?'"

Michael must have done just fine. His performance at the Grammy awards caused more people to go out and buy copies of *Thriller*. Before that time, *Thriller* had been the best-selling *solo* album of all time. In late March, it passed *Saturday Night Fever* as the best-selling record album of all time.

6

$\mathcal{M}$ichael Jackson, Incorporated

Joe and Katherine Jackson sat together in the audience at the Grammy awards ceremony. But they were no longer husband and wife. Although they were now divorced, they were on friendly terms. Joe Jackson felt free to visit the house in Encino whenever he wanted to. Katherine Jackson was still involved in the family businesses. Michael felt bad about his parents' divorce. He still loved them both. But there was no question about whose side he was on. He had always been closer to his mother, and once his father left, he became closer to her still. He was grateful to her for taking care of him for so many years. He wanted, now, to take care of her.

He decided to redecorate the whole house for her. He had it remodeled as a Swiss chalet. He had the walls painted and he bought new furniture. But he also had some remodeling done for himself—like the mini Pirates of the Caribbean ride. For his mother's birthday in the spring of 1984, he presented her with a red Rolls Royce, all tied up with a white ribbon.

Michael's disagreements with his father were about more than family matters. They were also about business. At the time the *Thriller* album was released, The Jacksons, including Michael, were under "dual management." Joe Jackson was their manager, as he had always been. But Joe Jackson had also hired a management company, Weisner/DeMann Entertainment, Inc., back in 1978 when he felt he needed help in dealing with Epic Records. That company's first contract with The Jacksons ended in March 1983 and Joe Jackson did not want to renew it. In explaining why to reporters, he made a point of mentioning that Weisner DeMann was a white company.

Michael did not like that at all. He told a reporter for *Billboard* magazine, "I don't know what would make him say something like that. To hear him talk like that turns my stomach. I don't know where he gets that from. I happen to be color-blind. I don't hire color; I hire competence. The individual can be of any race or creed as long as I get the best. I am president of my organization, and I have the final word on every decision. Racism is not my motto. One day I strongly expect every color to live as one family."

To be fair to Joe Jackson, he had gotten his color consciousness long before Michael was even born. He had grown up poor and had experienced a good deal of racism. He had worked hard to raise his children in an atmosphere that was protected from racism. He had done such a good job that Michael, for one, refused to accept that it even existed.

Michael knows that racism does exist. He feels that the habit of the music industry to categorize black records as "Rhythm and Blues" is racist. He did not like it at all when his album *Off The Wall* was nominated for the 1980 Grammys only in the Rhythm and Blues category. He thought it should have been nominated in the Pop category. For that reason, he refused to sing at any future Grammy Awards presentations, including the 1984 awards night, when he was nominated for so many Grammys. But Michael does not believe that it does any good to bring up the matter of racism, as his father did. He thinks it should be dealt with in private.

One thing Michael shared with his father was the importance of the family. That had not changed with the divorce. For Michael, that meant continuing to work with The Jacksons on occasion. When in mid-1983 his father asked him to do a 1984 tour with his brothers he agreed.

Michael's brothers, and two of his sisters, were still very active in the record business. Marlon had produced a hit single for singer Betty White. Janet had made an album and had appeared in a couple of TV series. In May 1984 she was hired as a regular on the series *Fame*. LaToya had recorded her third album. Jermaine had done a successful last album for Motown called *Let Me Tickle Your Fancy*. Then he had signed with a new record label, Arista, and started work on a new album. *Jermaine Jackson* was issued by Arista in the spring of 1984. He was also going to produce a video for singer Pia Zadora. Michael's brothers and sisters had talent and energy. But there was no question that Michael was the superstar of the family. He could help them a lot by working with them.

Michael wanted to help his family. But going on a tour with his brothers was not the way he would have chosen to help them. He didn't like touring. If he had to go on tour with his brothers, he would not have chosen the tour promoter they wanted. Don King was a promoter of boxing matches. But his father and his brothers wanted Don King. King had come to them with a "package deal" for a tour plus two commercials for Pepsi-Cola.

Electric-haired boxing promoter Don King announced The Jacksons'
Victory Tour. Michael took little Emmanuel Lewis of the *Webster* TV
show to the press conference. The pint-sized star also went to the Grammy
Awards with Michael.

So, Michael agreed to do a tour he did not want to do, with a promoter he did not want.

That was the son and brother Michael Jackson. The business-man Michael Jackson made sure certain requirements were written into the contract he signed. Most of them had to do with the quality of the act. He wanted control over the orchestra and the music and the dancing and the songs they sang. As far as the Pepsi commercials went, he insisted that he would not appear actually drinking Pepsi. He had nothing against the soft drink, but he did not want to be "used" to sell a product to that extent.

All the things Michael insisted on were put into the contracts before he and his family signed them. Don King then went to work setting up the tour. In the meantime, The Jacksons began filming the Pepsi commercials.

Both of the commercials were choreographed by Michael Peters, who had done the choreography for Michael's *Thriller* video. The first one shows The Jacksons walking down a city street and seeing a group of young kids who are singing and dancing. The leader of the group looks like a young Michael Jackson, and he is clearly imitating Michael when he bumps into the real Michael Jackson. Then The Jacksons sing and dance briefly with the youngsters.

The second commercial was to be even bigger. It would show The Jacksons as if they were in concert. Shooting was done in an actual auditorium, the Shrine Auditorium in Los Angeles, and 400 kids got free tickets to watch it. The rest of The Jacksons would be performing onstage, and Michael would come down a set of stairs, and out from a cloud of colored smoke, to join his brothers.

While filming a commercial for Pepsi-Cola in early 1984, Michael's hair was ignited in a fireworks explosion. Jermaine, whose back was to Michael, did not see it happen.

The smoke was created with flash powder. Merlin comets were used for flashes of light. During rehearsal of the part where Michael comes down the stairs, the technicians could not seem to get the smoke thick enough. They kept adding more flash powder and more Merlin comets. They set up another take. Michael started down the stairs. Suddenly there was a flash no one expected. The hair on the back of Michael's head was on fire! No one knows exactly what happened. Maybe a spark had hit him. Maybe the extreme heat inside the smoke cloud had caused some kind of spontaneous combustion.

Michael started screaming. His bodyguard, Miko Brando (son of Marlon Brando, the actor), tackled him to the floor and quickly put out the fire using his jacket. Then, Michael was rushed to the emergency room of Cedars-Sinai Medical Center. There, Dr. Steven Hoefflin, the plastic surgeon who had reshaped Michael's nose, examined him. The doctor arranged for Michael to be transferred to a special burn center.

As soon as the story of the accident hit the wire services, it was picked up by newspapers and radio and TV stations around the world. Thousands and thousands of teenagers wanted Michael to know that they were sorry about the accident and that they wanted him to get well quickly. Since most of them didn't have his address, they telephoned and sent letters to radio stations that played Michael's records. One Los Angeles radio station was getting 300 letters a day. It was like that around the world, according to Billy Kirkland. Kirkland, a song writer, wrote a song called "Dear Michael" using the letters. Other people bought copies of *Thriller* to show that they cared. The album sold a million copies in the four days after the accident.

Thanks to his bodyguard's quick action, Michael's injuries were not serious. He was conscious on the way to the hospital emergency room and insisted on keeping his one white glove on. There was a 3-inch to 4-inch circle of burned flesh on the back of his head, but it was treated and Michael was released from the special burn center just eighteen hours later. The spot was bandaged, and Michael wore a hat to cover it. Later, he had a small hairpiece made to cover the spot. In mid-April, Michael underwent laser surgery to reconstruct the burned spot. The doctor was able to stitch the wound without having to transplant or implant hair from other parts of Michael's head. The Pepsi commercial was edited so the accident was not in it and it was shown for the first time on Grammy Awards night, 1984. That meant that Michael not only walked off with the most awards ever given to one performer but also appeared during a break in the program. People in the business call that "saturation." By that is meant that he was everywhere.

MTV liked the commercial so much that they offered to show it without charging the usual advertising fees. They wanted to show it like a regular video.

The Pepsi commercials were just part of the work The Jacksons had to do in connection with their tour. They were going to record a new album, which would be released just before the tour began. They had to work out a complete concert stage act. The months between September of 1983, when they signed the contracts for the tour, and July of 1984, when the tour began, were busy for them all. In fact, they were too busy.

Each of The Jacksons had his own very definite ideas about music. Since they had not worked together for a while, they had to get used to being a group again. Michael is a perfectionist, and he insisted on being involved in every aspect of the album's

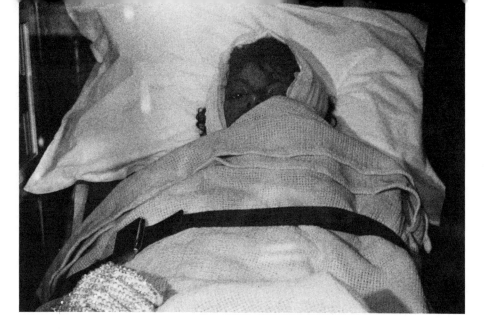

Michael suffered second-degree burns on his scalp, but he recovered quickly. Later, he had laser surgery to reconstruct the burned spot.

production. The other brothers wanted to be involved, too. But at last, in mid-May 1984, they finished the album, which they had decided to call *Victory*. It was scheduled for release in June. Its contents were a closely-guarded secret, but word had leaked out about a couple of the tracks. One was called "Buffalo Bill," and it was one of Michael's up-tempo dance compositions. People who had heard it raved about it. Another track was a duet between Michael and Mick Jagger of the Rolling Stones called "State of Shock," also written by Michael.

Meanwhile, they had started to rehearse their concert act in mid-April. They told their backup band that rehearsals would begin at 7 a.m. sharp. Their assistant coordinator reminded the band members that The Jacksons don't like drugs and would not stand for any drug use during the tour. Then they all went to work. Watching The Jacksons rehearsing was exciting in itself. So much musical knowledge and experience were in one rehearsal studio. James McBride of *People* spent a day with them in late May. "Each has more than fifteen years experience in the business, and among them they have sold some 150 million records," he wrote of The Jacksons. "Each can hear in his mind's ear the keyboard harmonies, the rhythm guitar licks, the synthesizer patterns, the drumbeats and bass hooks that create music up to the family standard." Sometimes they worked on a single number until 1 a.m. They all agreed that it had to be right.

The act included some of Michael's hits, like "Wanna Be Startin' Somethin'," some of Jermaine's songs, and some Jacksons songs, including several from the new album. There was very little bickering among the brothers, very little competition or jockeying for power. They all had the same goal: the best concert act they had ever done. Considering that they were badly pressed for time, rehearsals went very smoothly.

Unfortunately, the planning and promotion of the tour itself was not going smoothly at all. Everyone knew that The Jacksons' reunion tour could be the biggest money-maker in the history of the music business. When there is a lot of money at stake, there are usually problems. While Don King was still involved as tour coordinator, the promoter could not be decided on. Nearly twenty advisers were fighting for control of the tour. Until somebody came out on top, no definite decisions could be made about the tour route or ticket prices. Relations among The Jacksons were not as harmonious when it came to the *business* of the tour. In fact, they were split into three different camps: Michael's, his father's, and that of the other brothers. Each had their own attorneys and advisers.

By late May it was still not certain how many cities or which cities would be on the tour—or when it would even start. By then, some of the cities that had wanted to be included on the tour were having second thoughts. There had been so much hoopla. There was also so much disorganization that the cities in question wondered if the tour promoters and coordinators were capable of organizing the necessary security. A huge concert can very easily turn into an occasion for violence. After one of The Jacksons' big concerts in New York in 1981, youths had gone on a chain-snatching spree. And everyone remembered what had happened at Diana Ross's concert in New York's Central Park the previous summer. Dozens of youths had been arrested for muggings.

Michael found it all very distasteful. He personally kept away from the negotiations as much as possible, letting his representatives speak for him. When the brothers made appearances to promote the tour, Michael was often absent. He was worrying about "overexposure."

Overexposure is a great danger for a star. If he is seen in public too much, if his picture is too often in the paper and on buttons and T-shirts, if too many of his records are released too close together, the public can get tired of him. Michael did not want to be a "has-been" by the age of thirty. What bothered him most was that so much of the exposure he was getting because of the tour was beyond his control.

For his brothers, overexposure was not a problem. They welcomed all the publicity. As Jermaine told Marilyn Beck of the New York *Daily News*, "[Our names are] on the people's lips and the time to worry is when they stop talking about you." That was the real division between Michael and his brothers. The tour was the biggest opportunity of their careers. Michael just wanted to get it over with. When in late June the announcement finally came that The Jacksons' tour would begin July 6, 7, and 8 in Arrowhead Stadium in Kansas City, Missouri, Michael's main reaction was that at last the first step had been taken toward getting it over with.

The tour was all that it had been promised, and more. There were computerized fireworks, red and green lasers that fired the length of the stadiums and auditoriums, thunder, explosions, swirling smoke, a grand entrance trapdoor-platform-stairway, a sword being pulled from a stone just as in the famous myth. But Michael was the most astonishing special effect of all. As Gerri Hirshey wrote in *Rolling Stone*, he was "a human hydrofoil gliding through five costume changes and a dance bag of moonwalks, Marcel Marceau mime walks, spins, kicks, half turns and angular flash-frame poses." The audiences got their money's worth. In fact, The Jacksons' show was so full of show-biz razzmatazz that after they played Madison Square Garden, New York critics started comparing other big shows to it and finding them "skimpy" by comparison. All the worries about fan riots proved to be groundless. At every tour stop, the audiences were well behaved. No doubt the high ticket prices had something to do with it, for who would pay $30 and then act up? The ticket prices continued to cause grumbling throughout the tour, but Michael had very cleverly gotten himself out of that controversy by announcing that all his earnings from the tour would go to charity.

He did not like being on the defensive, as he was in the controversy over ticket prices, but he found himself in that position often during the mid- and late summer of 1984. The tremendous amount of publicity that attended the tour brought up all the old rumors about his plastic surgery and his sexuality. At last, Michael felt forced to respond to them. He called a press conference where a representative read a prepared statement that Michael hoped would put the rumors to rest: He was not a homosexual and he'd had no plastic surgery on his eyes.

Michael was relieved when the tour ended. He was glad to be out of the relentless glare of the public spotlight. All the planning for the *Victory* album and tour had taken a full year. He wanted to get on with his own career. He has said that he feels a responsibility to use his God-given talent by continuing to grow. He wanted to do new things. He saw all kinds of possibilities in video. It is an exciting new medium, and he liked the idea of working at something that was just beginning to develop. He also wanted to do movies, and in September 1984, he signed with Columbia Pictures to do two films. One was *They've Landed*, a movie-length version of the *Beat It* video featuring Michael and his brothers. The other film had not been decided on at the time.

A medium that does not interest Michael at all is stage acting. He would not want to do a Broadway show. The reason, he says, is that live stage performances live only as long as the show. Reminded that Broadway shows can be videotaped, he insists that it's not the same thing. "The actor's tense, he's being taped, and things aren't falling naturally," he explained to Bob Colacello of *Interview* in 1982. "That's what I hate about Broadway. I feel I'm giving a whole lot for nothing. I like to capture things and hold them there and share them with the whole world."

Michael is very concerned with saving moments in time. That's why he tape-recorded his conversations with Jane Fonda and Katharine Hepburn when he visited them during the filming of *On Golden Pond*.

Michael has formed several companies. One, called Experiments in Sound, is involved in the research and development of new sound technologies. Another, Optimum Productions, put together the *Thriller* video and documentary. He has his own publishing company. Not only does he publish his own songs, but also he has bought the catalogue of all the hits by Sly and the Family Stone and wants to buy other major catalogues. He may form a film company and produce his own movies. *Rolling Stone* magazine quoted an "insider" as saying, "When Michael does a film, it'll be a sort of musical Michael Jackson-meets-*E.T.*-and-*Star Wars*. It'll be a spectacular extravaganza, a futuristic musical with all sorts of special effects, bizarre choreography and fantastic music."

So, maybe one day E.T. will get a chance to go to Michael's house after all.

$\mathcal{D}$iscography

ALBUMS

Michael Jackson with the Jackson Five

Diana Ross Presents The Jackson Five (Motown 1969) †

ABC (Motown 1970) †

The Jackson Five Christmas Album (Motown 1970) †

Maybe Tomorrow (Motown 1971) †

Goin' Back to Indiana (TV soundtrack) (Motown 1971) †

The Jackson Five's Greatest Hits (Motown 1971) †

Lookin' Through the Windows (Motown 1972) †

Skywriter (Motown 1973)

Dancing Machine (Motown 1974) †

Moving Violation (Motown 1975)

Joyful Jukebox Music (Motown 1975)

The Jackson Five Anthology (Motown 1976) †

Boogie (Natural Resources/Motown 1979)

Motown Superstar Series Volume 12: The Jackson Five (Motown 1980)

Michael Jackson & The Jackson Five: Great Songs and Performances that Inspired the Motown 25th Anniversary Special (Motown 1983)

Michael Jackson with The Jacksons

The Jacksons (Epic/Philadelphia International 1976)*

Goin' Places (Epic/Philadelphia International 1977)

Destiny (Epic 1978)**

Triumph (Epic 1978)

The Jacksons Live (Epic 1981)

Victory (Epic 1984)

Michael Jackson

Got To Be There (Motown 1972)

Ben (Motown 1972) †

Music & Me (Motown 1973)

Forever, Michael (Motown 1975)

The Best of Michael Jackson (Motown 1975)

Off The Wall (Epic 1979) *

Motown Superstar Series Volume 7: Michael Jackson (Motown 1980)

One Day In Your Life (Motown 1981)

E.T.: The Extra-Terrestrial Storybook (MCA 1982)

Thriller (Epic 1982)**

SINGLES

Michael Jackson with The Jackson Five

I'm A Big Boy Now (Steeltown)

We Don't Have To Be Over 21 (Steeltown)

I Want You Back (Motown 1969) ††

ABC (Motown 1970) ††

The Love You Save/I Found that Girl (Motown 1970) ††

I'll Be There (Motown 1970) ††

Mama's Pearl (Motown 1971) †

Never Can Say Goodbye (Motown 1971) †

Maybe Tomorrow (Motown 1971)

Sugar Daddy (Motown 1971) †

Little Bitty Pretty One (Motown 1972)

Lookin' Through The Windows (Motown 1972)

Corner Of The Sky (Motown 1972) †

Hallelujah Day (Motown 1973)

Get It Together (Motown 1973)

Dancing Machine (Motown 1974) ††

Whatever You Got I Want (Motown 1974)

I Am Love, Part I and II (Motown 1975)

Forever Came Today (Motown 1975)

Michael Jackson with The Jacksons

Enjoy Yourself (Epic 1976)*

Show You The Way To Go (Epic/Philadelphia International 1977)

Goin' Places (Epic/Philadelphia International 1977)

Blame It On The Boogie (Epic 1978)

Shake Your Body Down To The Ground (Epic 1979)**
Lovely One (Epic 1980)
Heartbreak Hotel (Epic 1980)
Can You Feel It (Epic 1981)
Walk Right Now (Epic 1981)

Michael Jackson and Paul McCartney
The Girl Is Mine (Epic 1982)*
Say, Say, Say (Epic 1983)

Michael Jackson
Got To Be There (Motown 1971) †
Rockin' Robin (Motown 1971) †
I Wanna Be Where You Are (Motown 1972)
Ben (Motown 1972) ††
With A Child's Heart (Motown 1973)
We're Almost There (Motown 1975)
Just A Little Bit Of You (Motown 1975)
You Can't Win (Part I) (Epic 1979)
Don't Stop 'Til You Get Enough (Epic 1979)**
Rock With You (Epic 1979)*
Off The Wall (Epic 1979)
She's Out Of My Life (Epic 1980)*
One Day In Your Life (Motown 1980)
Thriller (Epic 1983)
Billie Jean (Epic 1983)*
Beat It (Epic 1983)*
Wanna Be Startin' Something (Epic 1983)*
Human Nature (Epic 1983)
PYT (Pretty Young Thing) (Epic 1983)

---

† Proclaimed "gold" for selling 500,000 copies by Motown but not certified as gold by the Record Industry Association of America.

†† Proclaimed "platinum" for selling 1,000,000 copies by Motown but not certified as platinum by the Record Industry Association of America.

* Certified gold for selling 500,000 copies.

** Certified platinum for selling 1,000,000 copies.